Beyond the Headlines:
The Academic Growth Story of Uvalde Students

Dr. Sandra Zuniga Garza

Disclaimer

The information contained in the book and its related guides serve as a part of the author's collection of books, which may increase their income passively. The material can include content from the third party, but the author takes full charge of quoting genuine resources (may be subjected to copyright). If the content inculcated in the publication becomes obsolete due to technical reasons or whatsoever, the author or the publication house are entitled to no blames. No part of this shall be reproduced, sold, or transmitted in any medium by the third party except after the author's approval.

Beyond the Headlines: The Academic Growth Story of Uvalde Students
Copyright © 2024 by Sandra Zuniga Garza
All rights reserved.
International rights secured.

No part of this publication may be reproduced, stored in a retrieval system, or transmitted in any form or by any means—electronic, mechanical, photocopying, recording, or otherwise—without the prior written permission of the copyright owner, except for brief quotations used in book reviews, educational materials, or scholarly articles.

ISBN: 9798998884016

First Edition: 2024

Printed in the United States of America

Table of Contents

Preface 1

Chapter 1 From F to B: The Journey of Transformation 4

Chapter 2 Captivation: Igniting the Love for Learning 11

Chapter 3 Discovering Potential: Unleashing Talent 21

Chapter 4 Personalization: Tailoring to Every Student 30

Chapter 5 Reflections on Growth: Cultivating a Culture of Improvement 37

Chapter 6 Inspiring Success: Setting and Achieving Educational Goals 44

Chapter 7 Data-Driven Decision Making: Fostering Student Agency and Academic Growth 51

Chapter 8 Building Foundations: Supporting New Teachers and Leaders for Educational Success 61

Chapter 9 Leading with Vision: Empowering a District to Achieve Transformation 68

Chapter 10 Resilience Amidst Tragedy: Honoring the Journey and Looking Forward 77

Acknowledgments 90

Most Valuable Players 91

About the Author 94

Dedication

To the teachers, leaders, and learners of Uvalde CISD:

May this book stand as a lasting tribute to your extraordinary achievements during the 2018–2022 academic growth era. You faced challenges that would have stopped many — but you chose to rise, to persevere, and to transform.

Let these pages remind you not just of what you have accomplished, but of the strength within you to rise again and again, no matter what lies ahead.

Preface

As I write these words, I am filled with pride, responsibility, and hope—feelings shaped by my experiences within the Uvalde CISD community. The journey I share here is not an abstract tale of educational transformation, but a deeply personal story rooted in Uvalde and Batesville, Texas—two interconnected communities I had the privilege to serve. While often overshadowed by larger headlines, this is a story that deserves to be told authentically by someone who lived it.

"Beyond the Headlines: The Academic Growth Story of Uvalde Students" chronicles a remarkable chapter in Uvalde CISD's history, marked by resilience, determination, and transformation in the face of adversity. In 2018, the district faced significant academic challenges, earning an F rating (59). Soon after, the COVID-19 pandemic exacerbated these struggles, bringing school closures, learning loss, and far-reaching impacts that extended well beyond the initial disruption. Yet, amidst these obstacles, the community rallied together, determined to rise above the challenges and create a brighter future for their students.

As someone who worked within the district during this time, I witnessed firsthand the unwavering commitment of educators, students, and families to persevere. Despite overwhelming challenges, their efforts led to an extraordinary academic turnaround—from an F rating in 2018 to a B rating (80) in 2022. This type of growth, particularly during the pandemic, was exceptional and not reflective of the average trends seen across the nation. It was a unique achievement, one that underscores the resilience, dedication, and innovation of the Uvalde CISD learning community.

The unprecedented 21-point increase in academic performance was more than a statistic; it was a testament to the power of collaboration and the belief in the potential of every student. Educators embraced new strategies and innovations, students rose to meet higher expectations, and families supported these efforts with trust and encouragement. This collective determination fostered a culture of continuous improvement and demonstrated that even in the most challenging circumstances, meaningful transformation is possible.

This book uncovers the untold story of how resilience, innovation, and the relentless pursuit of excellence made this transformation possible. It provides practical strategies and reflections that fueled the district's success, offering a roadmap for educators, administrators, and leaders striving to foster academic excellence in their own contexts. By exploring the lessons learned and challenges overcome, it highlights the impact of a united community working toward a common purpose.

My hope is that this book will inspire and guide those who believe in the transformative power of education. It is a tribute to the students, teachers, and families of Uvalde CISD who, united in purpose, achieved the extraordinary. It reminds us that even in the face of immense adversity, there is potential for resilience, growth, and lasting impact. Together, we can rise beyond the headlines, uncovering stories of hope, transformation, and the unyielding belief that every challenge holds the promise of a brighter future.

Chapter 1
From F to B: The Journey of Transformation

"In the middle of difficulty lies opportunity."
– Albert Einstein

In 2022, discussions about student performance were gaining attention across South Texas. While Uvalde CISD's 21-point academic growth was acknowledged, it understandably took a backseat to the profound tragedy that shook our community, claiming the lives of 19 children and 2 teachers. This heartbreaking loss deeply impacted all of us and naturally shifted the focus away from the district's academic achievements during that time.

Yet, the story of growth and resilience began just as the district braced for the unprecedented challenges brought by COVID-19 school closures. Against this backdrop, Uvalde CISD embarked on a journey of renewal. While many districts struggled for years to recover from learning loss, Uvalde CISD emerged not only resilient but with a record of fostering student growth. Now, the full story of this remarkable transformation can finally be told.

The Need for a Mind Shift

In 2018, during our continuous improvement processes, it became clear to me and other district leaders that a mindset shift was necessary. We realized that if we wanted to achieve different results, we had to embrace innovative approaches to teaching and learning. As a rural South Texas district, however, we often found ourselves grappling with the reality that our visions were limited by funding. I remember feeling both the excitement of what could be and the frustration of knowing our resources were stretched thin. Still, I knew we had to push forward. After closely exploring options, we managed to secure a series of state-funded grants through the Texas Education Agency's Blended Learning initiative – an opportunity that felt like a lifeline. These grants included funding for both planning and implementation in math and English language arts, providing the foundation we needed to begin transforming our classrooms.

Leveraging Partnerships and Grants

Through collaborations with external service providers, Uvalde CISD set out on a transformative journey to reshape teaching and learning. Recognizing the importance of including diverse perspectives, we aimed to engage all stakeholders in shaping this new instructional approach. The Teaching and Learning team initiated the formation of a design committee, which brought together district and campus administrators, teachers, school board members, community members, and, most importantly, our students. This inclusive approach ensured that every voice was heard in developing our new educational framework.

The Strategic Design Committee

The strategic design committee met for several consecutive days and was tasked with identifying core values and the ideal instructional framework for Uvalde CISD. The team shared countless ideas and eventually came to a consensus on a framework with five critical components. On the final day, it was the students who named the newly developed model, in honor of the Uvalde mascots, the coyotes and lobos: 'The Paw Print.' This framework became a powerful symbol of unity and the shared vision for innovative teaching and learning that our district community strived to achieve.

The Paw Print Framework

The Paw Print framework was designed to revolutionize teaching and learning, with the goal of cultivating engaged and self-directed learners. It comprised five key steps:

1. **Captivate**: Creating a safe, nurturing, and engaging environment that fosters creativity and self-expression.

2. **Discover**: Providing rigorous learning experiences that spark curiosity and promote autonomy and confidence in a risk-free environment.

3. **Personalize**: Offering personalized academic and social-emotional learning experiences, encouraging students to creatively explore and solve challenges.

4. **Reflect**: Enabling students to monitor, track, and assess their growth, empowering them to take ownership of their academic and emotional development.

5. **Inspire**: Encouraging students to share their knowledge, inspiring others to learn and grow, thereby deepening their own understanding and contributing to a supportive learning community.

Implementation of the Paw Print

With the framework established, the district began the complex process of bringing this vision to life. The implementation of The Paw Print required a multi-phase effort. First, teachers and administrators underwent extensive training on the new instructional framework. Next, the district integrated technology into classrooms, providing students with access to devices and online learning platforms. Teacher and student protocols were then developed, outlining expected actions and behaviors in this transformed learning environment. For teachers, this meant adopting differentiated instruction and project-based learning; for students, it meant taking an active role in setting goals and tracking progress.

Overcoming Challenges

Shifting the mindsets of teachers and students accustomed to traditional methods required time and effort. However, with ongoing professional development and the success of early adopters, the district gradually embraced the new approaches. Another challenge was ensuring equitable access to technology in our rural district, where not all students had access to high-speed internet. To address this, the district provided devices and worked with local internet providers to offer affordable options for families.

The Spring Break That Disrupted Efforts

Just as the district began implementing the Paw Print framework, Spring Break arrived. However, instead of returning to classrooms, Uvalde CISD—like schools across the country—was met with the sudden and unprecedented challenge of COVID-19 closures. The district quickly pivoted to ensure continued learning from home. Though the Paw Print framework was initially designed for in-person instruction, it became invaluable in guiding and structuring this new approach. Teachers, students, and parents embraced its structure, and the district swiftly adapted to provide virtual training and support.

Conclusion: Rising Above Adversity

The journey from an "F" to a "B" was not solely about academic scores; it was about a community uniting, redefining education, and demonstrating resilience in the face of unprecedented challenges. The Paw Print framework, conceived to foster engaged learners, became the backbone of Uvalde CISD's response to crisis. It provided structure, support, and a path forward when the world was turned upside down.

As we close this chapter, we reflect on how Uvalde CISD not only adapted to a rapidly changing landscape but did so with a clear vision and unwavering determination. The district's ability to navigate the complexities of virtual learning while keeping the needs of students and teachers at the forefront is a testament to the power of strategic planning, community collaboration, and innovative thinking.

Reflective Questions for Educators:

- How can your team foster a culture of resilience in the face of challenges?
- In what ways can you engage others in a shared vision for academic success?
- What frameworks or systems could you implement to provide structure and support for teaching and learning?
- As a leader, how do you foster a balance between academic priorities and the emotional and social needs of students and staff?
- What lessons can be learned from past disruptions to enhance strategic planning?

Chapter 2
Captivation: Igniting the Love for Learning

"If children feel safe, they take risks, ask questions, make mistakes, learn to trust, share their feelings, and grow."

– Alfie Kohn

Driving Uvalde CISD's transformative journey was a profound commitment to captivation—placing students' interests at the forefront of the instructional framework. I remember thinking that, at its core, this approach highlighted what teaching was really about: connecting with students on a personal level and sparking their curiosity. For many of us, this shift reinforced a fundamental truth we had always known—teaching is most powerful when it hooks students and draws them into the learning process. It wasn't just about teachers delivering information anymore; it was about making learning something that students wanted to engage with.

Shifting from Teacher-Directed to Student-Centered Learning

Before this paradigm shift, Uvalde CISD classrooms predominantly followed a teacher-directed model. Observations revealed that lessons often involved lectures and direct instruction to the entire class. Even when activities were 'hands-on', they sometimes lacked the depth or rigor needed to fully engage students and be 'minds on'. This traditional approach, where the teacher was the primary source of knowledge, tended to limit opportunities for student engagement and personalization.

Recognizing the need for evolution, teachers and administrators explored various educational models. They studied The Fundamental Five, which offered valuable strategies like framing lessons and utilizing power zones to enhance teaching effectiveness. They also investigated the 4 C's framework, which emphasizes collaboration, communication, critical thinking, and creativity. While these models provided important insights, the focus remained largely on refining teaching practices rather than shifting the emphasis to student-centered learning and outcomes.

The Role of Professional Learning Communities (PLCs)

The implementation of this new system was integral to the district's transformation. It established a robust support network that connected the teaching and learning team with instructional coaches, teachers, and students, creating a well-oiled machine of collaborative effort. Principals were deeply engaged, ensuring seamless integration and operation across all aspects of the system.

Previously, Professional Learning Communities (PLCs) in the district had been primarily focused on planning and revisiting pre-existing units of study. These PLCs often lacked a clear, outcome-driven agenda, which limited their effectiveness. However, the new system introduced a more dynamic approach. It shifted the focus of PLCs towards outcomes and continuous improvement, fostering a culture of collaboration and accountability that significantly enhanced the overall educational experience. When circumstances limited face-to-face interactions, it was common to see PLCs meeting regularly via Zoom or at home dining room tables across the city.

Leveraging Technology and Digital Tools

In an era where digital natives are increasingly shaping the educational landscape, Uvalde CISD embraced technology to enhance learning. Teachers capitalized on the district's 1:1 iPad initiative, tapping into a wealth of digital resources to engage students. Initially, they chose tools that were interactive, game-like, and animated to captivate students' attention.

As educators grew more skilled in leveraging these technologies, they began to see the transformative potential of student-led learning. They recognized that empowering students to set their own goals and take ownership of their learning journey not only motivated them but also fostered a sense of true agency. This shift was not just about using digital tools for engagement but about redefining the role of technology to support and amplify student-driven educational experiences. The result was a more dynamic and responsive learning environment that harnessed the full potential of digital innovation to inspire and engage students in unprecedented ways.

Real-World Connections and Student Engagement

A vital strategy in fostering a genuine love for learning involved making real-world connections and demonstrating the relevance of education. By transforming abstract concepts into tangible, real-life experiences, lessons became more meaningful and engaging. For example, a math lesson on area and perimeter was brought to life through a connection to architecture, allowing students to see how architects apply these principles in their work. Similarly, science lessons on ecology were enriched by having students investigate local environmental issues and participate in a community river clean-up project.

Integrating these real-world connections not only made the content more relevant but also sparked greater student interest and engagement. Teachers observed that when students could see the practical application of their learning, their motivation soared. This approach turned lessons into dynamic, interactive experiences, reinforcing the idea that education is not just about acquiring knowledge but about understanding its impact and application in the world beyond the classroom.

Building Curiosity and Stronger Relationships

Curiosity emerged as a central element in the classroom, driving a shift toward more personalized and engaging lessons. Teachers began to explore their students' interests and passions, which helped to tailor lessons and foster deeper connections. This approach not only enhanced student engagement but also strengthened the relationships between students and teachers, making students feel more valued and understood. Instead of being passive recipients of information, students became active participants in their learning journey.

The transition to this new approach was gradual. Change didn't happen overnight; it began with a few early adopters who embraced and experimented with these new methods. As these pioneering teachers shared their experiences and successful strategies with their colleagues, the culture of curiosity and engagement gradually spread. This collaborative environment allowed for the continuous refinement and implementation of best practices. Over time, this culture of sharing and mutual support played a crucial role in the overall success of the transformation, with more teachers progressively adopting and integrating these innovative approaches into their own classrooms.

The Power of Student-Led Learning

As teachers mastered the art of captivation, they noticed a shift in their classrooms. Students began to take ownership of their learning, setting goals, and working towards achieving them. This sense of agency empowered students to become self-motivated learners who were invested in their educational journeys.

Student-led learning also encouraged critical thinking and problem-solving skills. Instead of merely following instructions, students started becoming involved in designing experiments, leading discussions, and exploring topics that interested them. This active engagement not only enhanced their understanding but also built confidence and independence.

Overcoming Challenges and Celebrating Wins

The journey towards captivation was not without its challenges. Transitioning from a teacher-directed to a student-centered approach required a significant shift in mindset and practice. Teachers had to become facilitators and guides rather than lecturers, which involved rethinking their roles and embracing new strategies.

However, the successes far outweighed the challenges. Classrooms became vibrant spaces where students were excited to learn. Teachers reported higher levels of student engagement and motivation, and academic performance improved as a result. The focus on student interests and real-world connections made learning more meaningful and enjoyable for everyone involved.

Sustaining the Momentum

Maintaining the momentum of this transformation required a steadfast commitment to ongoing professional development and support. The district's dedication to investing in training and resources was unwavering, always aligned with the evolving needs of students, teachers, and administrators. Regular PLC meetings became a platform for sharing experiences, discussing challenges, and celebrating milestones, fostering a culture of continuous growth and collaboration.

To keep tabs on change efforts, the district kept student voices at the heart of the process. By actively seeking feedback through surveys and focus groups, they ensured that the transformation remained responsive and relevant. This feedback loop was not just a mechanism for assessment but a testament to the district's commitment to honoring student perspectives and adapting to their needs.

In this way, the district did not just sustain the momentum; it nurtured a dynamic and evolving learning environment. The commitment to listening, learning, and evolving was a powerful reminder that transformation is a journey, not a destination, and that every step forward is driven by a shared vision of excellence and student success.

Conclusion: A Journey of Engagement and Growth

The transformative journey of Uvalde CISD exemplifies the profound impact that a focused commitment to captivation can have on education. By shifting from a traditional, teacher-directed model to a dynamic, student-centered approach, the district not only redefined teaching practices but also reignited a passion for learning among students.

The evolution from early adopters to a widespread culture of curiosity and engagement illustrates that meaningful change is a gradual process. It requires patience, collaboration, and a willingness to embrace new methods and technologies. As teachers and students alike adapted to this new way of learning, they discovered that true educational success lies in creating environments where students feel valued, understood, and empowered.

Through leveraging technology, making real-world connections, and fostering strong relationships, teachers demonstrated that learning is most effective when it resonates with students' interests and experiences. The district's commitment to professional development and responsive feedback ensured that the transformation remained aligned with its original vision and was focused on empowerment.

As we reflect on this chapter, it becomes clear that the heart of this transformation was a shared vision of excellence and a dedication to student success. The district's journey underscores a powerful truth: that by placing students at the center of the learning experience and continuously evolving to meet their needs, we can cultivate an educational environment where curiosity thrives, engagement flourishes, and every student is inspired to reach their full potential.

Reflective Questions for Educators:

- How can you create a learning environment that captivates student interest and fosters engagement?
- How can you shift from a teacher-led approach to a learner-centered model?
- How can you use technology to empower students to take ownership of their learning?
- What real-world connections can you make to show students the relevance of their studies?
- How can you build relationships with learners to understand their interests and personalize their learning?

Chapter 3
Discovering Potential: Unleashing Talent

"The greatest danger for most of us is not that our aim is too high and we miss it, but that it is too low and we reach it."

— Michelangelo

Following Captivation, the next crucial step in the Paw Print framework was Discovery—a concept that deeply resonated with me as we continued to reshape our district's approach to learning. After capturing students' attention, it was essential to give them opportunities to dive deeply into tasks and explore their own curiosity. I vividly remember the excitement I felt when I saw teachers embracing this shift, moving beyond traditional content delivery to foster true student engagement. It was inspiring to witness how this phase of discovery laid the foundation of a learning space where student autonomy could flourish.

Shift to Student-Centered Learning Plans

To foster student centeredness, Uvalde CISD transitioned from traditional teacher lesson plans—primarily for teachers' use—to developing student-facing learning plans. Instructional strategies were no longer merely listed; they were presented as challenges for students, complete with hyperlinked resources to facilitate learning and project completion. This approach empowered students to take charge of their own learning journeys and to incorporate a level of choice into their pathway.

Transition from Traditional to Discovery-Based Learning

The transition from traditional classroom instruction to a discovery-based model was not simply a change in techniques, but a shift in mindset for both teachers and students. In the past, the classroom revolved around the teacher as the central authority, delivering content through lectures and directing the learning process. I remember observing these settings where students, though attentive, were passive recipients of information, with few opportunities to explore topics on their own or ask deeper questions.

However, with the introduction of discovery-based learning, students transformed into active participants. I saw firsthand how their roles shifted—they became investigators and problem-solvers, empowered to ask questions and seek answers. In one classroom, instead of a lecture on ecosystems, students were tasked with creating their own mini-ecosystems and answering questions like, "How do plants convert sunlight into energy, and why is this process vital for life on Earth?" It was fascinating to watch as students delved into their projects, asking real-world questions and engaging with the material on a deeper level. Teachers were no longer just authorities; they became guides, helping students navigate this journey of inquiry and reflection.

Effective questioning was another essential part of this shift. I remember sitting in on a lesson where, instead of asking students to recite facts about photosynthesis, the teacher posed open-ended questions: "What if plants couldn't perform photosynthesis? How might life on Earth be different?" These types of questions fostered critical thinking and encouraged students to connect the material to broader concepts.

What made this approach even more impactful was how it tapped into students' intrinsic motivation. As they worked on projects, standards-aligned, formative assessments were integrated naturally, allowing students to track their progress and see how their skills were growing. This sense of ownership over their learning sparked engagement, and it was clear that they were genuinely invested in improving their proficiency in various Texas Essential Knowledge and Skills (TEKS).

Walking into classrooms during this period, I often saw students immersed in hands-on activities at learning stations, collaborating with peers to solve real-world problems. These stations created dynamic learning environments where students could apply knowledge in practical ways, catering to diverse learning styles and keeping them actively involved.

Perhaps the most exciting element of this shift was the introduction of student choice. By giving students a say in their projects, teachers were able to align lessons with students' personal interests, fueling curiosity and engagement. I remember one student who was passionate about renewable energy, and his science project evolved into a mini research paper on how solar panels could be integrated into school facilities. This type of personalized learning helped students make meaningful connections to the material and fostered a deeper love for learning.

As we implemented discovery-based learning across the district, there were valuable lessons learned. Teachers discovered the need to balance structure with flexibility, offering enough guidance to keep students on track while allowing room for creativity. Scaffolding techniques became important tools, as teachers provided initial support before gradually giving students more independence.

Creating a culture of trust and respect was another key element. By fostering a growth mindset, teachers were encouraged to take risks, and students were encouraged to learn from mistakes and view challenges as opportunities for growth. This shift from a fixed mindset to a growth mindset allowed students to see learning as an ongoing journey rather than just a series of tasks to complete.

Over time, these critical elements became part of the process of planning and support that took place in the daily Professional Learning Communities (PLCs). We witnessed these teams of teachers and teacher leaders come together with intentionality and energy.

Practical Example: A Unit on Ecosystems

To illustrate the implementation of discovery-based learning, let's consider a unit on ecosystems. Instead of the traditional, teacher-facing lesson plan, learning plans with embedded resources to foster autonomy were created to guide students.

Learning Plan for Students

1. **Captivate**: Students are provided some overarching guiding questions for the unit of study and watch a linked video on ecosystems to show an authentic, real-world connection.

2. **Discover**: Students are challenged with creation of a project. By this point, teachers have already planned in PLCs what a performance rubric might look like. To create the rubric, they have considered, "What can a student at each performance level do? (Does Not Meet

Grade Level Standards, Approaches Grade Level Standards, Meets Grade Level Standards, and Masters Grade Level Standards). This 'keeping the end in mind' tool allows students to see for themselves which performance level they want to aim for, and provides a roadmap they can follow as they strive to meet their goal.

3. **Personalize**: Students are provided rubrics, project guidelines, and exemplary models. They use these to create their own mini-ecosystems. Hyperlinked articles, videos, and interactive simulations on ecosystems and photosynthesis are also provided.

    - **Research Station:** Students use digital libraries and educational websites to gather information.
    - **Creation Station:** Students build their mini-ecosystems using provided materials.
    - **Collaboration Station:** Groups discuss their observations and hypotheses.
    - **Technology Station:** Students engage with digital, standards-based questions related to the science concepts being studied. This station provides teachers with real-time data on

student learning progress and offers students an opportunity to document their own learning progress.

- **Teacher-Led Small Group:** This station allows the teacher to meet individually with students to review data, discuss progress, and set goals. It also provides the opportunity for the teacher to work with small groups of students who need additional support or challenge.

4. **Reflect:** Students write journal entries to answer project questions and reflect on their findings. They are also presented opportunities to reflect on their progress on overall science standards being studied. Data folders are updated and students are able to answer, "Where did I do well? Where can I do better? What is my goal moving forward? What can I do to reach that goal?"

5. **Inspire:** Students have an opportunity to share learning with peers, with parents, with teacher and in some cases, beyond the classroom walls.

Conclusion: Empowering Learners for a Brighter Future

The journey to discovering and unleashing student talents through discovery-based learning is transformative. By shifting from traditional, teacher-directed models to student-centered approaches, teachers created an environment where students were empowered to explore, inquire, and take ownership of their learning. Effective questioning, intrinsic motivation, and personalized learning plans fostered critical thinking, self-direction, and a love for lifelong learning. The implementation of stations, scaffolding techniques, and a culture of trust and respect ensured that students were supported and encouraged to reach their full potential. As students became confident and autonomous learners, they felt better prepared to navigate new experiences, equipped with the skills and mindset necessary for continuous growth and success.

Reflective Questions for Educators:

1. How can you integrate discovery-based learning to promote student autonomy and critical thinking?
2. What strategies can you implement to foster effective questioning that leads to deeper inquiry and understanding?
3. How can you balance structure with flexibility, allowing students to explore their interests while meeting personally set learning goals?
4. What steps can you take to develop a culture of trust and respect that encourages students to take risks and learn from mistakes?
5. How can you personalize learning plans to align with student interests while maintaining academic rigor?

Chapter 4
Personalization: Tailoring to Every Student

"Tell me and I forget. Teach me and I remember. Involve me and I learn."
— Benjamin Franklin

Over the years, I have seen firsthand how education has evolved from a one-size-fits-all approach to one that celebrates each student's unique journey. For me, this shift was not just about changing the way we teach—it was about recognizing each learner's potential and finding ways to nurture it. I remember the first time I saw personalized learning transform a classroom, turning it into a space where every student felt understood and supported. These moments reinforced my belief that education should always be about meeting each learner where they are. Personalization, the next step of the Paw Print framework, guided our district's commitment to ensuring that each student receives the support and opportunities they need to thrive.

Shifting to Personalized Pathways

The journey towards personalization began with a fundamental realization: every student is unique. Teachers, empowered by continuous Professional Learning Communities (PLCs), became skilled in identifying not only the tier of each student but also their specific needs in relation to state and federal accountability. This deep understanding allowed for the creation of tailored educational experiences that addressed each student's requirements and learning styles.

Professional Development and Accountability

Teacher training focused extensively on addressing the needs of struggling learners, advanced learners, and special populations. This training included strategies and monitoring techniques that ensured all students received the support they needed. There was a concerted, district-wide effort to simplify state accountability measures so that campuses, planning teams, classroom teams, and even individual students could use the state's methodology for student achievement to arrive at a "Magic Number".

The Magic Number aligned with current measures, providing a quick way for teachers and learners alike to monitor progress toward set goals. It was common to walk into campuses and see data walls displaying current progress, new goals, and celebrations of achievements. This practice kept momentum going and supported the data-driven culture critical to the transformation. This was always part of the growth mindset and any data measures were never punitive in any way. The fostering of this safe environment was a game-changer to the new mindset and data-driven culture.

Implementing Personalized Pathways

In the classroom, personalized pathways took several forms:

- **Small Group Instruction:** Teachers provided targeted instruction to small groups, addressing specific knowledge gaps and skill areas.

- **Differentiated Stations:** Students engaged in stations tailored to their needs, either through pre-determined teacher-created activities or student-chosen tasks based on their interests and needs.

- **Blended Learning:** The integration of blended learning platforms allowed students to interact with TEKS-based content, providing real-time data that guided teachers in grouping students for additional support or enrichment.

Planning and Reflection

Effective implementation of personalized learning required thoughtful planning and reflection. Teachers focused on several critical questions:

- What are the different stations and activities for this unit?

- How can students use standards-based, online playlists to guide their own learning?

- What formative assessments will I use to gauge student understanding?

- How can assessments be aligned with STAAR features to prepare students?

- What strategies will be employed to assess group work and provide feedback?

- How will progress be monitored by students and how will I provide feedback regularly?

- What resources will students be using for research, learning, formative assessments, data tracking?

- How can students be encouraged to contribute resources and suggest additional materials?

- How will students be guided in effectively using these resources?

Support and Mentorship

District specialists and instructional coaches played an essential role in this transformation, offering guidance and support to teachers as they adopted personalized learning strategies. By addressing the key questions and implementing effective planning protocols, educators created a learning environment that was both responsive and supportive of each student's journey.

Conclusion: The Power of Personalization in Education

As education continues to evolve, the shift toward personalization represents a profound transformation in how we approach teaching and learning. By moving beyond the one-size-fits-all model, educators can embrace the uniqueness of each student, tailoring educational experiences to meet their individual needs and aspirations.

This leg of the journey proved that personalized pathways are not merely an instructional strategy but a commitment to recognizing and nurturing the distinct potential within every learner. Through small group instruction, differentiated stations, and blended learning, teachers created environments where students were not only recipients of knowledge but active participants in their educational journeys.

Professional development and accountability measures, such as The Magic Number played crucial roles in this transformation. By simplifying complex state measures and fostering a safe, growth-oriented environment, schools turned data into a tool for empowerment rather than a source of pressure.

The thoughtful planning and reflection that underpinned personalized learning ensured that educators were not only meeting their students' academic needs but also supporting their emotional and personal growth. The support and mentorship provided by district specialists and instructional coaches were vital to guiding this shift, helping teachers implement effective strategies and create responsive learning environments.

The impact of personalization in this chapter of the district's story was profound. It created a more inclusive, engaging learning environment where students could thrive academically and emotionally. By embracing and refining personalized learning practices, educators laid the foundation for students to unlock their full potential. This chapter has highlighted the transformative power of personalization, showing how it can reshape both learning experiences and outcomes. It is clear that personalization will continue to be central to effective, equitable education, ensuring that every student has the opportunity to excel and grow in their own way.

Reflective Questions for Educators:

1. How can you create personalized pathways to meet the diverse needs of all your students?
2. What role can data play in helping you tailor instruction to individual student needs without creating pressure or anxiety?
3. How can you use small group instruction or differentiated stations to provide more targeted support for students?
4. What strategies can you employ to ensure that personalization addresses both academic growth and students' emotional and personal development?
5. How can professional development and mentorship support your efforts to implement personalized learning effectively?

Chapter 5
Reflections on Growth: Cultivating a Culture of Improvement

*"The greatest glory in living lies not in never falling,
but in rising every time we fall."*
— *Nelson Mandela*

Growth has always been a central focus in my work as an educator. I have seen firsthand how creating a data culture of self-reflection, empowerment and continuous improvement can truly transform students' academic development. At Uvalde CISD, I remember feeling inspired by the way we introduced the Paw Print Educator and Learner Protocols—a framework designed not only to engage students academically but to help them develop the skills needed for self-reflection and ownership of their learning. This next step of the Paw Print—reflection—enabled students to monitor, assess, and take ownership of their own growth. Watching students embrace this approach made it clear how reflection, alongside personalized learning, could shape not only academic success but also emotional resilience.

Shifting from Traditional to Student-Centered Reflection

In traditional classrooms, reflection was often limited to the grades and feedback provided by teachers. Student progress was communicated through grades, which offered a narrow view of a student's learning journey. However, the new reflective process at Uvalde CISD shifted ownership of learning to the students themselves. This shift was accomplished through strategic design and the implementation of systems that supported a more comprehensive and inclusive approach to student reflection.

Commitment at the District Level

The district's commitment to fostering a culture of improvement began with providing teachers continuous time to plan and grow professionally. This dedicated time in Professional Learning Communities (PLCs) allowed teachers to create stations and small groups, share successful instructional strategies with colleagues, and continuously refine their teaching methods.

Moreover, the district ensured that classrooms were equipped with updated technology, allowing students to interact with standards-based digital learning tools. These platforms, aligned with Texas Essential Knowledge and Skills (TEKS), provided real-time data on student performance for each standard. The access to immediate feedback transformed how teachers and students approached learning and reflection.

Data-Driven Instruction and Student Agency

The introduction of progress dashboards allowed teachers to continuously monitor student learning. However, the true innovation in this instructional model was that students were also given access to this real-time data, enabling them to set their own goals and track their progress. By adopting a blended learning approach, the district designed a systemic process that went beyond simply accessing data; it actively engaged both teachers and students in using the information to inform their next steps.

For teachers, the data identified student groups that required additional support. For instance, if several students struggled with understanding a particular concept, the teacher could use this real-time data to form a small group for targeted intervention. This data-driven instruction ensured that teaching was responsive and tailored to students' needs. Teachers no longer had to wait for formal assessments; they could adjust on the fly, ensuring that each student received the precise support they needed to succeed.

For students, having access to their performance data encouraged self-reflection and goal setting. Students used data-tracking folders and dashboards to plot their progress, evaluate whether they had met their goals, and set new objectives. This transparency fostered a sense of responsibility and investment in their own learning journey. Watching their progress unfold in real-time ignited intrinsic motivation, pushing them to seek new ways to improve.

Rather than waiting for teacher direction, students began to identify learning opportunities for themselves—whether through accessing additional resources, collaborating with peers, or seeking guidance from their teachers. This process became less about passively receiving information and more about active, self-driven learning, as students took charge of their educational growth and found personal satisfaction in their achievements.

The result was a classroom culture where both teachers and students became partners in the learning process, continuously using data to drive success. Students were not just passive participants—they were empowered, motivated learners who sought new opportunities to grow academically and emotionally.

Classroom Implementation

In the classroom, the shift towards a reflective culture was evident. Students engaged in station rotations as part of the blended learning model, while teachers interacted with small groups, pulled students for data-driven instruction, or met one-on-one to discuss goals and progress. This strategic design fostered an environment where students were deeply invested in their learning. Walking into a classroom, it was common to see students proudly sharing their progress with teachers and peers. Conversations with students revealed their excitement about meeting goals and their eagerness to show their data folders, filled with visual representations of their growth. The once-familiar groans of "Do we have to take a test?" were now replaced with "Can I try the assessment again? I know I can meet my next goal!"

Building a Reflective Culture

The district's commitment extended beyond the classroom. Campus administrators played a crucial role in fostering this reflective culture. They engaged with students during classroom visits and conferences, encouraging them to share their progress and celebrate their achievements. This practice not only reinforced the importance of reflection but also strengthened the bond between students and school leaders.

By embedding reflection into the educational process, the district shifted the mindset from one where teachers solely held responsibility for student learning to one where students actively participated in their educational journey. This cultural shift was not just about academic growth but also about nurturing a sense of ownership, responsibility, and self-awareness in students.

Conclusion: Growth through Self-Reflection

Reflections on growth were essential for cultivating a culture of improvement. By empowering students to monitor, track, and assess their progress, Uvalde CISD created an environment where learners took ownership of their academic development. This systemic approach, supported by continuous professional development for teachers and the integration of technology, ensured that the reflective process was meaningful and impactful. As students became more invested in their learning, they were better equipped to seek the resources and support needed to grow, leading to a more enriching educational experience.

Reflective Questions for Educators:

1. How can you incorporate student-centered reflection practices that encourage learners to take ownership of their academic progress?
2. What tools or strategies can you use to ensure that students have real-time access to their data and are equipped to use it for goal-setting and self-assessment?
3. How can professional development for teachers foster a culture of continuous reflection and improvement within your institution?
4. What role can leaders play in supporting a reflective culture and encouraging students to take pride in their growth?
5. How can you create an environment where data is used, not only for accountability, but for student-driven learning?

Chapter 6
Inspiring Success: Setting and Achieving Educational Goals

> *"The future belongs to those who believe in the beauty of their dreams."*
> — *Eleanor Roosevelt*

In the vibrant and dynamic classrooms of Uvalde CISD, I witnessed firsthand a revolution in learning. Students were no longer just absorbing knowledge passively; they were actively sharing their discoveries, sparking inspiration among their peers, and fueling a collective desire to learn and grow. Inspiration, the final step of the Paw Print framework, was evident as students motivated each other to reach new heights through sharing their learning, presenting, and crushing their goals. This chapter outlines strategies teachers employed to foster inspiration.

The Power of Sharing Knowledge

Students were provided countless opportunities to share their newly acquired knowledge with their peers. This practice not only reinforced their own understanding but also allowed classmates to offer input, ask questions, and deepen their collective learning. In these interactions, learning became a communal activity, where each student's success contributed to the overall growth of the group. Sharing knowledge fostered a collaborative environment that nurtured critical thinking, creativity, and communication skills—key competencies for success in the modern world.

In one classroom, students worked on a project about environmental conservation. After conducting their research, each student presented their findings to the class. These presentations were not just about displaying what they had learned; they were invitations for others to engage, question, and contribute. As students discussed and debated, they built on each other's insights, expanding their perspectives and developing a richer, more comprehensive understanding of the topic. The collaborative process also encouraged students to take ownership of the material, as they realized their voices and ideas were valued by their peers.

This exchange of knowledge also inspired a sense of community and shared responsibility for learning. As students learned from one another, they became more invested in each other's success, fostering an environment where collaboration, rather than competition, drove academic achievement.

The Role of Teachers in Inspiring Learning

Teachers played a crucial role in this educational paradigm. They designed and implemented processes that fostered student showcasing and the presentation of new learning. By structuring the learning environment to support these activities, teachers ensured that students were not only recipients of knowledge but also active participants in their educational journey.

To provide structure and accountability, teachers equipped student presenters with performance rubrics aligned with the Texas Essential Knowledge and Skills (TEKS) standards. These rubrics ensured that presentations were not only informative but also intentional, guiding students to focus on key learning objectives and communicate their knowledge effectively. As a result, students learned to present their ideas in a way that not only demonstrated mastery of the content but also engaged their audience, fostering an environment where both the presenters and their peers deepened their understanding of the material.

Teachers structured lessons to include opportunities for students to present their work. They incorporated higher-order questioning techniques to push students to think deeply about the material, challenging them to go beyond surface-level understanding. During one-on-one conferences, teachers mentored students through their challenges, helping them explore complex concepts with more depth and clarity. This personalized approach ensured that every student—whether they were struggling or excelling—was supported and encouraged to grow. Through these practices, teachers created a classroom culture where learning was shared and collaborative, and students were equipped with the tools to teach and learn from each other.

Aligning Learning with Curriculum Standards

Alignment with the Texas Essential Knowledge and Skills (TEKS) was a cornerstone of the educational strategies at Uvalde CISD. Teachers designed learning opportunities that pushed students to meet the required benchmarks, ensuring that the content was relevant and aligned with current educational expectations. As these practices evolved, a formal process built around TEKS alignment began to take shape—this became known as the Instructional Assessment Protocol, a backward design system that ensured all learning activities connected to the required standards and outcomes.

This backward design approach meant that teachers started with the end goals in mind—the desired student outcomes as defined by TEKS—and worked backward to plan lessons, assessments, and learning activities. This PLC-grounded system created a clear and intentional path for both teaching and learning, making sure that every step of the instructional process was focused on helping students achieve mastery.

Clear learning targets established and articulated in student-centered language. Statements like "I will" and "We will" helped students understand the objectives of each lesson and demonstrated the gradual release of responsibility in the learning process. This clarity helped focus student efforts, providing them with a roadmap to track their progress and meet the established goals.

Continuous Assessment and Support

Assessment was an ongoing process, directly linked to the established learning targets. Teachers used various types of standards and depth appropriate exit tickets to gauge student understanding at the end of each lesson. These tickets offered students multiple ways to demonstrate their grasp of the material, providing a comprehensive view of their progress.

To enhance student success, additional enrichment, remediation, and support were provided. Resources were available to help students, whether they required extra assistance with concepts or were ready for advanced challenges.

Fostering Lifelong Learning

The goal of inspiration was to foster a lifelong passion for learning. Students applied their knowledge in community projects, such as environmental clean-ups, linking classroom learning to real-world impact and fostering a sense of responsibility.

Conclusion: Empowering Success through Goal-Setting and Real-World Learning

Uvalde CISD's approach succeeded by inspiring students to set and achieve ambitious goals. Through knowledge sharing, structured support, and alignment with state standards, teachers created an environment where students thrived. Extending learning beyond the classroom and promoting lifelong learning empowered students to become engaged, active members of their classroom learning communities.

Reflective Questions for Educators:

1. How can you design a process that empowers students to set and achieve meaningful, self-driven goals that inspire personal growth?
2. What strategies can you implement to encourage collaborative knowledge sharing that sparks curiosity and fosters deeper understanding among students?
3. How can you create authentic, real-world learning opportunities that inspire students to connect classroom concepts to their lives and future ambitions?
4. In what ways can continuous assessment and reflection help students not only track their progress but also ignite a sense of ownership and motivation to reach new heights?
5. How can you cultivate a culture of lifelong learning that inspires students to apply their knowledge in impactful ways beyond the classroom?

Chapter 7
Data-Driven Decision Making: Fostering Student Agency and Academic Growth

"What gets measured gets improved."
— Peter Drucker

In today's educational landscape, the concept of student agency has become more than just a theory—it is something I have witnessed firsthand in classrooms. Student agency, the ability for students to make independent choices about their learning, became a transformative force at Uvalde CISD during this growth era. I remember seeing the shift in students as they began to take charge of their academic journey, empowered by access to real-time data that showed them exactly where they stood and where they could grow. In a data-driven environment, students were not passive recipients of knowledge anymore—they became active participants. This empowerment fostered a sense of ownership over their learning that I had never seen before, and the resulting academic growth was both meaningful and profound. This chapter delves into how the students of Uvalde benefitted from a data-driven approach that emphasized their agency in setting and achieving goals, with the support of teachers, district leadership, and technology integration.

Evolution of Data: From Adults to Students

Traditionally, data analysis in schools is an adult-centric process, primarily involving teachers and administrators. Data is used to make decisions about curriculum, instruction, and student interventions, with little involvement from the students themselves. However, a significant shift occurred in Uvalde, where the data culture evolved to include students in the process. Students now understood their own data, which empowered them to take charge of their academic progress. This shift transformed the way students approached learning, as they became more engaged and motivated to achieve their goals.

The involvement of students in setting and monitoring their academic goals had a profound impact. Students were no longer passive learners but active participants who had had been empowered to track their progress, identify areas for improvement, and seek out resources to help them succeed. This new data culture led to a positive learning environment where students were eager to showcase their progress and to take ownership of their learning.

The Role of Teachers in Supporting Goals

Teachers played a crucial role in facilitating student agency by helping students set attainable academic goals and monitoring their progress. In Uvalde and Batesville, teachers adopted strategies that allowed students to engage with their data meaningfully. For example, teachers guided students in creating personal data trackers, where they recorded their performance on assessments and tracked their progress over time. These trackers served as a visual representation of their growth and motivated students to set and achieve their goals.

Regular progress monitoring was essential in this process. Teachers frequently reviewed student data and provided feedback, allowing students to make adjustments to their learning strategies. This ongoing support ensured that students remained focused on their goals and continued to make progress. The collaborative effort between teachers and students in goal setting and monitoring contributed to a culture of continuous improvement and academic success.

Implementation Levels District-Wide

The implementation of data-driven decision-making varied across different educational levels and from campus to campus. At the elementary level, generally speaking, the approach reached a mid-high level of implementation, where students actively engaged with their data and set goals. Elementary students embraced the use of data trackers and classroom data walls, which displayed class goals and progress. These visual tools made data accessible and understandable for younger students, fostering a sense of ownership and pride in their achievements.

At the secondary level, data-driven practices also made significant strides and the approach reached a mid-level of implementation. Secondary students showed gains in engaging with their data and began to incorporate it into their learning strategies. One freshman student was quoted as seeking additional resources to deepen her understanding after analyzing her data. This proactive approach demonstrated a growing sense of agency and adaptability among secondary students, reflecting ongoing progress and commitment to their academic growth.

Although implementation varied across grade levels and campuses, it was noticeable that classrooms with higher student agency were the ones regularly sharing their wins—daily, with parents and the community, often through social media. When the district analyzed data on high-growth classrooms, it was interesting to note that those celebrating gains using student data trackers, data walls, and PLCs were the ones where most students achieved at least a year of academic growth by year's end.

District Leadership and Support through PLCs

District leadership played a pivotal role in the successful implementation of data-driven decision-making. Leaders ensured that teachers received comprehensive training and ongoing support to integrate data into their teaching practices effectively. Additionally, they were strategic in selecting digital learning platforms that aligned not only with state standards but also with the need for student-facing data.

Professional Learning Communities (PLCs) were central to this process, providing a collaborative space where teachers could share successes, strategies, and challenges. Through these daily PLCs, educators worked together to develop tools such as student data trackers, which fostered student agency and ownership of learning.

The support from district leaders and the structure of PLCs established a solid foundation for data-driven practices. Teachers felt empowered to explore innovative strategies and grew more confident in using data to guide instruction. This collaborative approach also cultivated a powerful sense of community among educators—all 'rowing in the same direction'—working towards common goals. Moreover, the district strategically recruited specialists to provide in-person support during PLC sessions, offering guidance to both instructional coaches and teachers as they implemented these practices.

Collaborative Data Tracking and Goal Setting

In classrooms with high levels of implementation, collaborative data tracking and goal setting became the norm. Students, teachers, and planning teams worked together to set individual and "Magic Number" goals at the individual, classroom, and team levels. For example, students used personal data folders to track their progress, while classrooms had data walls that displayed class goals and achievements. In PLC rooms, teams set and monitored their goals, creating a shared sense of purpose and accountability.

These collaborative practices had a significant impact on student motivation and achievement. When students saw their progress displayed visually and understood how their efforts contributed to class and team goals, they were more likely to stay engaged and motivated. The emphasis on collaboration also encouraged students to support one another, creating a positive and inclusive learning environment.

Leveraging Technology and Standards-Based Platforms

The district's 1:1 iPad initiative was a game-changer in making data accessible to students and teachers. With access to standards-based learning platforms, students worked on specific skills and received immediate feedback on their performance. Teachers, in turn, accessed real-time data to identify students who needed reinforcement, those who were on track, and those who needed to be challenged. This data-driven approach allowed for differentiated instruction, where teachers tailored their lessons to meet the diverse needs of their students.

The integration of technology also made it easier for students to track their progress and set goals. For example, students used digital tools to create data trackers, set reminders for their goals, and monitor their achievements over time. The use of technology not only enhanced the learning experience but also empowered students to take an active role in their education.

Teacher-Led Small Groups and Differentiated Instruction

One of the most significant benefits of a data-driven approach was the ability to differentiate instruction based on student needs. Teachers used data insights to form small groups of students who required similar levels of support or challenge. In these teacher-led small groups, instruction was tailored to address specific areas of need, whether it was reinforcing a concept, providing additional practice, or offering enrichment opportunities.

The use of small groups proved to be highly effective in promoting student growth. Students received more personalized attention and instruction, which helped them to grasp difficult concepts and make progress toward their goals. Additionally, small groups provided a supportive environment where students could learn from one another and work collaboratively to achieve success.

Promoting a Growth Mindset and Celebrating Progress

A key component of the data-driven approach in Uvalde and Batesville was the promotion of a growth mindset. Instead of focusing solely on achieving a fixed score, the emphasis was on continuous improvement and effort. This shift in mindset was instrumental in creating a positive learning environment where students—and teachers alike—felt encouraged to take risks, make mistakes, and learn from them.

Celebrating progress, no matter how small, is a crucial aspect of this approach. Teachers and students alike recognized and celebrated achievements, whether it was mastering a new skill, improving a test score, or making progress toward a goal. These celebrations not only boosted student morale but also reinforced the importance of perseverance and hard work.

Conclusion: Harnessing Data for Empowered Learning

As Uvalde CISD continued to refine and expand its data-driven practices, several emerging trends and strategies held promise for the future. One such trend was the increased use of personalized learning pathways, where students could choose their own learning paths based on their interests, strengths, and areas for growth. Another was the integration of standards-based learning tools that provided deeper insights into student performance and helped educators make more informed decisions.

To sustain and expand data-driven practices, it was essential to continue providing teachers with the necessary training and support. Ongoing professional development, collaboration through PLCs, and the sharing of best practices were crucial in ensuring that data-driven decision-making remained a central part of the educational process district-wide.

Ultimately, the goal was to foster a learning environment where every student could take charge of their education, set and achieve personal goals, and experience meaningful academic growth. By prioritizing student agency and data-driven decision-making, the district positioned itself to realize this vision effectively.

Reflective Questions for Educators:

1. How can you foster a data-driven culture that empowers students to take ownership of their learning; while ensuring they understand the relevance of the data they're using?
2. What specific strategies can you implement to help students engage meaningfully with their data, set realistic goals, and continuously track their progress toward those goals?
3. How can you design collaborative data tracking and goal-setting practices that support both individual student growth and broader class-wide objectives?
4. In what ways can you leverage technology to support differentiated instruction effectively?
5. How can you use data to promote a growth mindset in students, encouraging them to view data as a tool for motivation, reflection, and continuous improvement, rather than as a measure of fixed outcomes?

Chapter 8
Building Foundations: Supporting New Teachers and Leaders for Educational Success

"A good leader inspires people to have confidence in the leader; a great leader inspires people to have confidence in themselves."
— Eleanor Roosevelt

Building capacity has always been a cornerstone of my educational journey. Whether working with pre-service and in-service teachers as a university faculty member, transforming schools through the National Center for Accelerated Schools, or leading learning in rural, disadvantaged districts, my focus has consistently been on empowering others to thrive. These experiences have shown me firsthand how crucial support—particularly for new teachers—is in fostering a strong and sustainable educational environment.

At Uvalde CISD, we quickly recognized that nurturing and guiding new teachers was not just important—it was essential for their success and that of their students. Like many communities, Uvalde and Batesville faced challenges in staffing classrooms with certified personnel. In response, we partnered with experts from the Education Service Center - Region 20 and other external organizations to provide formal training, onsite support, and personalized coaching for new educators. This collaboration ensured our new teachers received the mentoring and resources needed to align with the district's personalized learning goals.

Watching these educators grow in confidence and skill reaffirmed for me the transformative power of the right support. It not only accelerates their professional development but also enhances the academic progress of the students they serve.

Structured Induction Programs

At Uvalde CISD, the induction program for new teachers was designed to provide a structured and supportive introduction to the school environment. This program included back to school orientation sessions for beginning teachers (those new to the profession) and their mentors. It also included ongoing professional development for both teachers and mentors in the form of Zoom during school closures, afterschool/weekend training sessions, and onsite, in-classroom support. New teachers participated in workshops covering essential topics such as classroom management, instructional strategies aligned to the Paw Print, data-driven instruction, and technology integration.

The structured induction process aimed to ease the transition for new educators by offering them a clear roadmap and a network of support. This approach not only helped new teachers acclimate to their roles but also provided them with practical tools and resources to begin their teaching journey effectively. The collaboration with these partners was instrumental in tailoring these programs to meet the unique needs of beginning teachers in the region.

Mentorship and Coaching

A cornerstone of the support system was the mentorship program. Experienced teachers were paired with new educators to offer guidance, advice, and support. Mentors played a vital role in helping new teachers navigate the challenges of their first year, providing insights into effective teaching practices, and offering emotional support.

In addition to the support provided by their mentors, new teachers received personalized feedback, observed classroom practices, and were offered strategies for improvement by external trainers and coaches. This collaborative relationship between new teachers, mentors, and coaches fostered a supportive learning environment that contributed to the overall success of the new educators.

Professional Learning Communities for New Teachers

New teachers were integrated into their own Professional Learning Communities (PLCs) to benefit from the collective knowledge and experience of their colleagues. These PLCs provided a platform for new teachers to share their experiences, discuss challenges, and seek advice from veteran educators. Regular meetings and collaborative sessions allowed new teachers to engage in professional dialogue, receive constructive feedback, and participate in continuous learning.

The PLCs also offered opportunities for new teachers to observe and learn from their peers. By participating in classroom observations and lesson study groups, new teachers gained valuable insights into effective teaching strategies and classroom management techniques.

The formal training sessions with trainers via Zoom, afterschool and on weekends, also made for a powerful cohort and PLC in itself. It was common for beginning teachers to lean on them and on each other for emotional support as they doubted whether they were cut out to be a teacher.

Integration of Leadership Development

In addition to the robust support for new teachers, Uvalde CISD recognized the importance of strong leadership at the campus level. The district also sought leadership development support from Education Service Center Region 20. The leadership consultant helped lead Principal Professional Learning Communities (PLCs) to offer formal training sessions and provide executive coaching for individual campus leaders. Their involvement was crucial in equipping principals with the skills and confidence needed to lead their campuses through this period of significant change, ensuring that the district's vision was effectively implemented at every level.

Feedback and Continuous Improvement

In addition to collaborative learning opportunities and coaching conversations, regular feedback became a cornerstone of the support system for both new teachers and leaders. Onsite observations and one-on-one meetings with mentors, coaches, and principal evaluators provided ongoing, constructive feedback on performance. This continuous feedback loop empowered educators and leaders to reflect on their practices, set targeted goals for improvement, and consistently refine their approaches.

The emphasis on continuous improvement fostered confidence and promoted a growth mindset among new teachers and campus leaders. By recognizing their strengths and addressing areas for development, they were better equipped to succeed in their roles and positively impact their students' academic progress.

Conclusion: Investing in New Teacher and Leadership Success

The approach Uvalde CISD implemented was innovative, offering multiple touchpoints throughout the capacity-building process. The support system was diverse, including a variety of interactions such as online and onsite sessions, synchronous and asynchronous learning, one-on-one meetings, small learning communities, coaching conversations, mentor training, and emotional support. This comprehensive and multifaceted strategy ensured that new teachers and campus leaders received the tailored assistance they needed to thrive.

Supporting new educators and leaders is essential for fostering a thriving educational environment. Uvalde CISD's holistic approach—combining training, coaching, Professional Learning Communities (PLCs), and access to essential resources—ensured that they were well-prepared to succeed in their roles. By investing in their development, the district laid a strong foundation for ongoing excellence in education, which contributed directly to the overall growth and achievement of its students.

Reflective Questions for Educators:

1. What key components do you offer new educators (both teachers and leaders) to ensure their smooth transition into your environment?
2. How can mentoring be structured to provide both professional guidance and emotional support to new educators?
3. What types of external partnerships can you invest in to offer personalized, person-centered support for your new teachers, mentors, and leaders?
4. How can leadership development programs help district and campus leaders effectively implement initiatives and navigate periods of change?
5. How can you leverage internal and external expertise to cultivate and realize the vision you hope to instill?

Chapter 9
Leading with Vision: Empowering a District to Achieve Transformation

"Leadership is not about being in charge.
It's about taking care of those in your charge."
— Simon Sinek

In education, true transformation begins with leaders who not only envision a better future but actively inspire those around them to pursue it. At Uvalde CISD, the superintendent of schools embodied this visionary leadership, deeply rooted in the district's core values and unwavering commitment to its people. His approach was not just about managing change but about driving meaningful, long-lasting impact through intentional actions that resonated with every student, teacher, and administrator.

His leadership was anchored in four foundational pillars: enrichment, inclusivity, socio-emotional supports, and graduation. These weren't just ambitious goals—they were guiding principles that influenced every decision made and initiative undertaken in the district. Under his direction, Uvalde CISD adopted the motto "Believe in U." It was more than just a phrase; it was a living testament to his belief in the potential of every individual within the district. Every interaction, whether with students, educators, or community leaders, reflected his deep trust in their abilities and his commitment to their growth.

By fostering an inclusive, person-centered environment where everyone felt valued and empowered, the superintendent's leadership transcended expectations and set a new standard for what was possible in public education.

Empowering the Entire District Team

The superintendent's vision extended beyond academic leadership, reaching every corner of the district. He understood that systemic change required a collective effort, where each member of the district team played a crucial role in the transformation.

Not everyone was on board when the opportunity to apply for state funding for this effort came about. It was the superintendent who ultimately gave his blessing, with complete trust, not only in the academic team, but on other key players who would come to be critical supports to the movement.

The Teaching and Learning Team

The talent recruited to the Teaching and Learning team were also empowered to use their gifts. Through this process came two major game-changers:

1. Implementation of a digital learning culture – Several innovative initiatives were launched by our first

Blended Learning Specialist to foster professional learning, including:
   a. Teacher badging program
   b. Virtual summer conference
   c. Paw Print Pause Podcast
   d. Video tutorials
   e. Blended Learning Ambassador Program
2. Development of the Instructional Assessment Protocol (IAP) – A protocol was designed by our Grades 3-6 Curriculum Specialist to continue to support the ongoing implementation of change efforts. Among many of the strategies for fostering student agency and personalized learning, IAP included, but was not limited to, the following:
   a. Conditionally-formatted zone maps for growth data
   b. Instructional response to readiness, supporting, and highly tested standards
   c. Teachers' interactive folders with personalized student data for goal-setting
   d. Use of Texas Formative Assessment Resource for student practice in a state testing environment

Information Technology (IT)

Significant support came from the district's IT team, led by a Director whose expertise was both exceptional and multifaceted. With a deep understanding of networks, hardware, software, data management, and the complexities of the Public Education Information Management System (PEIMS), he brought a rare combination of skills to this growth era. This comprehensive knowledge, as well as his can-do mindset, allowed him to strategically guide the teaching and learning teams through seamless transitions between in-person, virtual, and hybrid learning environments.

His leadership, coupled with the dedication of his small but highly efficient team, went above and beyond traditional IT support. The team ensured that teachers and students had seamless access to essential devices, learning platforms, and a robust infrastructure that supported uninterrupted instruction. Beyond providing basic technical support, they were proactive in anticipating challenges, conducting system upgrades, and troubleshooting issues before they could disrupt the learning experience.

One of the most notable contributions was their ability to manage the district's data systems with precision. This attention to detail not only ensured that student data remained secure and accessible but also played a vital role in driving data-informed decision-making across the district. Their work allowed the district's leadership to act swiftly and effectively on key initiatives, optimizing outcomes in real-time.

The IT team's role extended into professional development, connecting staff with Apple partners, and equipping teachers with the digital tools and skills needed to enhance instruction and student engagement. They also provided critical technical support during virtual professional learning sessions, ensuring that educators could focus on their growth without technology hiccups. This comprehensive, behind-the-scenes work by the IT department was a cornerstone of the district's ability to adapt to evolving educational demands.

Grant Management and Parental Support

The district's Federal Programs Director played an instrumental role in the success of Uvalde CISD's transformation, ensuring that resources were strategically allocated to support the district's ambitious goals. With her expertise in grant management, she helped to secure and coordinate various funding streams, enabling the district to implement and sustain key initiatives. Whether through federal, state, or local grants, her skillful navigation of these processes allowed the district to maximize financial resources for the benefit of both educators and students.

Her contributions extended far beyond financial oversight. As a key player in strategic planning, she ensured that every funding source aligned with the district's broader vision of academic growth and inclusivity. By collaborating closely with campuses, she ensured that they each received the necessary attention and funding. Her efforts were crucial in designing personalized learning initiatives that met the unique needs of every student, reinforcing the district's commitment to inclusivity and equity.

Moreover, she was adept at managing the complexities of compliance and reporting associated with federal programs, ensuring that Uvalde CISD met all regulatory requirements while maintaining the flexibility to adjust resources as new needs arose. This level of oversight not only ensured accountability but also provided the district with the ability to adapt and respond to emerging challenges, all while staying focused on its mission of academic excellence.

Through her diligent work, the Federal Programs Director helped lay a sustainable foundation for Uvalde CISD's transformational initiatives, empowering the district to continue its path toward long-term success.

Special Populations

The success of Uvalde CISD's transformation also hinged on the invaluable support and collaboration provided by the

Directors of Special Education and Bilingual Education. These leaders played a crucial role in advancing the district's mission by supplying essential data about special education, bilingual, migrant, and dual language students, allowing the district to tailor its personalized learning initiatives effectively.

The Special Education Department demonstrated exceptional innovation by creating their own set of "look-for's" to guide special education co-teachers in developing student-centered instructional designs. This proactive approach ensured that instructional practices were personalized and tailored to meet the individual needs of students, making the co-teaching model both impactful and aligned with the district's vision for inclusivity. Their focus on empowering educators to deliver personalized, student-driven education was instrumental in guaranteeing that all students, regardless of ability, received high-quality, engaging learning experiences.

The Bilingual Department initially focused on the successful launch of the district's first-ever Dual Language Academy, a critical step in expanding opportunities for both English and Spanish native speakers. As the academy took shape, the department gradually incorporated key elements of the district's transformation, such as standards-based data tracking and other student-centered components. Their participation provided important insights and laid the groundwork for future growth in supporting bilingual and dual language students, aligning with the district's broader vision for inclusivity and academic excellence.

Together, these efforts by the Directors of Special Education and Bilingual Education ensured that the district's inclusive vision was not only aspirational but also actionable, making significant strides toward educational equity for all students.

Conclusion: Leading with Trust and Empowerment

The empowerment of the district team was a key factor in driving the transformation, but the true heroes who were beautifully empowered in this journey were the students and their teachers. This collective effort led to remarkable outcomes, as the campus and district teams worked together to create an educational environment that aligned with the four pillars and the overarching motto of "Believe in U."

Reflective Questions for Educators

1. How can you refine your leadership approach to create a culture of empowerment across all levels, even during challenging times?
2. What steps can you take to better align every department with the overall vision and goals, especially when facing resistance or lack of coordination?
3. How can you rebuild trust and foster empowerment within your leadership teams to initiate systemic transformation, even if morale or engagement is low?
4. How can personalized learning initiatives be strengthened or restructured to ensure that all students are included in your vision for success, particularly if current efforts are falling short?
5. How can you reinvigorate a motto or core set of values, like 'Believe in U,' to inspire and unify your school or district, especially when there is a lack of motivation or alignment with the common goal?

Chapter 10
Resilience Amidst Tragedy: Honoring the Journey and Looking Forward

"There is no greater agony than bearing an untold story inside you."
— *Maya Angelou*

The year 2022 was poised to be a culmination of years of hard work, dedication, and transformative progress for Uvalde CISD. The district had witnessed remarkable academic growth, fostered a culture of continuous improvement, and built a resilient community committed to the success and well-being of its students. Classrooms buzzed with excitement and engagement, teachers collaborated seamlessly, and students took ownership of their learning in unprecedented ways.

However, amidst these anticipated triumphs, an unimaginable tragedy struck on May 24, 2022, when a mass shooting at Robb Elementary School claimed the lives of 19 children and 2 teachers. This horrific event sent shockwaves through the community and the nation, casting a shadow over the district's remarkable achievements. Yet, in the face of profound grief and adversity, the spirit of resilience and unity that had been cultivated over the years became the cornerstone for healing and moving forward.

The Pinnacle of Academic Excellence

In the months leading up to May 2022, Uvalde CISD was experiencing one of its most successful academic years, energized by a renewed focus on growth and resilience following the challenges of school closures. The district had made remarkable progress, improving its state rating from a 59 (F) in 2018 to a 77 (C) in 2019. This achievement reflected the collective efforts of students, teachers, administrators, and community stakeholders. With this momentum, the district looked forward to further growth in its first, post-pandemic state rating.

Classrooms throughout the district were vibrant and engaging, with students meeting and crushing their goals daily. They were experiencing academic growth in core subjects, and you could feel the excitement of student ownership as you walked the campuses. The Paw Print framework had evolved into a well-developed and effective instructional model that seamlessly integrated engaging lessons, discovery-based learning, personalized pathways, reflective practices, and opportunities for students to inspire and lead. Blended learning celebrations flooded the UCISD Curriculum and Instruction Facebook page. The Instructional Assessment Protocol could be seen in every PLC. The teaching and learning process was in a good place.

Teachers had become facilitators of learning, employing data-driven strategies to customize instruction for diverse student needs. Professional Learning Communities (PLCs) thrived as centers of collaboration, innovation, and shared leadership, contributing to a cohesive and supportive educational environment.

Strengthening Community Partnerships

The district's success was further bolstered by robust community partnerships. Local businesses, organizations, and families were deeply involved in supporting educational initiatives, extracurricular activities, and student well-being programs. Community events celebrated student achievements and fostered a strong sense of pride and belonging among residents of Uvalde and Batesville.

Parental engagement had reached new heights, with families actively participating in school activities, volunteering, and collaborating with educators to support student learning and development. This collective effort created a nurturing and empowering environment that underscored the adage, "It takes a village to raise a child."

Loyal and True

Extracurricular programs flourished, offering students countless opportunities to explore their interests, develop talents, and build lasting friendships. Sports teams saw unprecedented success, with more state qualifiers than ever before. The number of qualifiers was so significant that a special board meeting was convened just to recognize all the student-athletes. Fine arts programs also reached new heights, with theater, band, and mariachi ensembles achieving remarkable accomplishments, shining in the spotlight, and further enhancing the district's reputation for excellence. These successes not only contributed to well-rounded student development but also reinforced a strong sense of pride and unity across the community, embodying the spirit of Uvalde's school song and long-standing motto, *Loyal and True*.

The Day That Changed Everything

On May 24, 2022, the Uvalde community was forever changed by a senseless act of violence at Robb Elementary School. The shooting resulted in the heartbreaking loss of 19 innocent children and 2 dedicated teachers, plunging the community into deep sorrow and shock. The tragedy resonated across the nation, eliciting widespread grief, empathy, and calls for action to prevent such atrocities in the future.

The immediate aftermath was characterized by overwhelming emotions—grief, anger, confusion, and despair—as families mourned their loved ones and the community grappled with the enormity of the loss. The tragedy tested the very fabric of the community, challenging the resilience and unity that had been so carefully cultivated over the years.

Immediate Response and Support

In the face of devastation, the Uvalde community drew upon its pre-existing foundation of emotional and social-emotional support. For years, the district had invested in fostering a culture of care, providing students and staff with access to counseling services and social-emotional learning (SEL) programs, such as Positive Behavior Interventions and Supports (PBIS). These efforts had long been integrated into the district's fabric, preparing both students and staff to navigate personal challenges. When tragedy struck, these existing structures became critical lifelines. Counselors, psychologists, and social workers quickly mobilized, expanding their reach to offer grief counseling and mental health services. The strength of Uvalde's response was not built overnight; it was the product of years of intentional planning, demonstrating that the district's long-standing focus on well-being laid the groundwork for its resilience during this most challenging time.

Community members rallied together, organizing vigils, memorials, and support networks to honor the victims and provide comfort to those affected. The outpouring of support extended beyond Uvalde, with people from across the country and around the world expressing condolences, offering assistance, and standing in solidarity with the grieving community.

Faith-based organizations, local businesses, and nonprofit groups played crucial roles in providing resources, hosting support events, and facilitating healing processes. The collective response underscored the depth of compassion and resilience within the community, showcasing humanity's capacity to come together in times of profound tragedy.

Healing and Rebuilding: The Path Forward

In the wake of the tragedy, Uvalde CISD placed a heightened emphasis on mental health and emotional well-being. The district expanded counseling services, implemented trauma-informed practices, and provided extensive support for students, staff, and families navigating the complex and ongoing process of grief and healing.

Professional development for educators included training on recognizing and addressing trauma, fostering supportive classroom environments, and integrating social-emotional learning into daily instruction. These efforts aimed to create safe and nurturing spaces where students could express their feelings, process their experiences, and find comfort and support among peers and trusted adults.

The 2022 Accountability Rating

Despite the profound challenges, Uvalde CISD remained steadfast in its commitment to providing high-quality education and opportunities for all students. The district recognized that continuing its mission was a vital part of honoring the lives lost and fostering hope for the future.

Three months after the tragedy, the news finally arrived: Uvalde students and teachers had achieved a state accountability rating of 80 (B), marking a remarkable 21-point growth from 2018's 59 (F). Under any other circumstances, such a milestone would have warranted a celebration of the collective efforts that led to this achievement. However, this was no time for celebration. The district was missing some of the teachers and students who had worked just as hard to earn this progress. As the superintendent poignantly stated, "I would have rather kept the 21 lives than the 21 points."

The Enduring Power of Community

The experiences of 2022 underscored the profound strength and resilience of the Uvalde community. In the face of unimaginable loss, the community's unity, compassion, and determination served as a beacon of hope and a foundation for recovery and growth.

The collaborative efforts of students, educators, families, and community members demonstrated that collective action and mutual support can pave the way toward healing and renewal even in the darkest times. These bonds, forged through shared triumphs and tragedies, continue to shape the community's identity and guide its path forward.

Inspiring Hope and Future Generations

As the Uvalde and Batesville communities move forward, the lessons learned from both its achievements and its hardships continue to inspire hope and guide future endeavors. The experiences lived by students, teachers, parents, staff, and leaders offer valuable insights into the importance of resilience, community engagement, and a holistic approach to education.

This story hopes to contribute to a broader conversation about educational transformation, community strength, and the capacity to overcome adversity. The narrative serves as an inspiration to other districts and communities, illustrating that through unity, dedication, and compassion, it is possible to navigate challenges and emerge stronger.

Conclusion: A Legacy of Strength and Unity

The academic growth story of Uvalde CISD is one of remarkable transformation, profound loss, and enduring resilience. The district's journey reflects the complexities of the human experience—the interweaving of joy and sorrow, success and struggle, hope and despair.

Through years of dedication to both educational excellence and the emotional well-being of its students, Uvalde CISD built a strong foundation that enabled the district to weather even the most unimaginable challenges. The district's response to tragedy not only showcased the strength of its people but also reinforced the power of forward-thinking leadership, community partnerships, and a shared vision for growth.

Today, the Uvalde community remains loyal and true to its students and learning community. This story captures a unique era of transformation—a time when dedicated leaders and educators came together, overcame immense challenges, and achieved remarkable academic progress. The legacy of that era, built on collaboration, vision, and a deep belief in every student's potential, stands as a testament to what is possible when people unite around a common purpose.

It is my hope that future leaders honor the hard-earned lessons of the past and recognize the profound contributions of those who drove this transformation. To dismiss or diminish these efforts would risk undoing the progress so many fought to achieve. Failing to honor these transformational heroes is not only unjust but also a disservice to the students and families who benefited from their work.

As the Uvalde and Batesville communities continue their journey, may they carry forward the values that fueled this era of growth: resilience, compassion, and an unwavering commitment to empowering future generations. This legacy stands as a beacon of hope, reminding us that even in the face of profound adversity, communities can come together to heal, grow, and build a better future.

May this story continue to inspire all who believe in the power of education to transform lives and unite communities.

Reflective Questions for Educators

1. How can your district or school foster a culture of resilience that not only prepares students and staff to face challenges, but also empowers them to grow stronger through academic, emotional, and unexpected difficulties?
2. What bold steps can be taken to ensure that your district's vision remains not only aligned with academic excellence and emotional well-being, but also becomes a guiding force for transformation?
3. How can your district's community partnerships be reimagined and strengthened to not only support student success and emotional recovery, but to also foster a deeper sense of unity and purpose in times of adversity?
4. How can educators and leaders celebrate progress while also compassionately addressing the emotional needs of their community, transforming moments of change into opportunities for renewed hope?
5. In what ways can the lessons from Uvalde CISD's journey ignite your passion to strengthen your team's capacity for educational transformation and resilience, inspiring others to follow in your footsteps?

Acknowledgments

First and foremost, to God, whose grace and guidance have been my constant source of strength throughout this journey.

To my husband, Celso—thank you for your love, support, and for standing by my side through every challenge and triumph.

To my son, Freddy, and daughter-in-law, Linda, your faith and strength inspire me daily. Your encouragement has been a pillar of support in my life.

To my precious grandchildren, Giancarlo, Camila, and Ace, you are the light of my life. I dedicate this work to the future you will help shape with your joy, curiosity and love.

To my beloved parents, Berta and the late Ricardo Zuniga, my brother Rick (Veronica), and my sister Julie (Ricardo), along with my nephew Ritchie and nieces Arianna and Alejandra—thank you for reminding me every day that family is where the heart grows.

A special thank you to Mary, Debra, Rose, and the many friends who checked on me daily during the darkest times. I could not have made it through without your care and friendship.

Most Valuable Players

This story would not have been possible without the incredible system of support we built together. I am deeply grateful to Dr. Hal Harrell for his leadership and vision, which were instrumental in the academic transformation of Uvalde CISD. To the School Board and the community Strategic Design Team, thank you for your trust, input, and support. To the principals, assistant principals, and instructional coaches—your commitment was vital to this historic success.

My heartfelt thanks go to the Uvalde CISD Teaching and Learning team for their dedication to students and staff. Special recognition goes to Jennifer Griffin for developing the Instructional Assessment Protocol and operationalizing 'The Magic Number' for accountability-aligned practices, Natalie Arias for her outstanding work with blended learning during home instruction and the transition back to campus, Julie Hipp for laying the foundation with early learners, Rachel Hohman for leading the transformation in the secondary classrooms, Blair Dorris for strengthening intervention and enrichment systems, and both Sandra Gonzales and Alicia Bradley for ensuring our Gifted and Talented students remained challenged.

I am deeply appreciative of Senior Staff and Central Office for their contributions to the blended learning initiative that drove growth during this era—especially Norma Carranza (Federal and State Programs), whose above-and-beyond expertise in coordinating and managing state resources was invaluable, and the leaders who ensured our special populations also transitioned to personalized learning: Victor Baron (Special Education), who developed clear look-fors in co-teach classrooms, and Dr. Mario Ferron, who launched the district's first Dual Language Academy. Special thanks goes to Cash Keith (Technology) for his unmatched expertise in networks, hardware, software, data, and PEIMS, all of which were critical to supporting academic growth. It could not have been done without his support and that of his Project Manager, David Zamora, Jr.

I also extend my gratitude to our external partners from the Texas Education Agency, with special appreciation for Andrew Hodge, Associate Commissioner of Systems Innovation, and Education Service Center Region 20, led by Executive Director Dr. Jeff Goldhorn.

Heartfelt thanks go to Jayme Presley and Marie Riley for their personalized support of beginning teachers and mentors, and to Michael Torres for his leadership development tailored to district initiatives. You each became part of the UCISD family, and your impact will always be remembered.

I would like to recognize John Fessenden from Lead4Ward for providing tools that aligned our practices with accountability, Engage2Learn for guiding planning and implementation, Renaissance Learning for teaching us how to measure and track true growth, and Nelson Taylor from Apple for his exceptional coaching. Each of you played a key role in driving academic progress.

Lastly, my deepest gratitude goes to the true heroes in our classrooms: the UCISD teachers, paras, and students. Their courage, dedication, and partnership made this journey possible. Together, they achieved something remarkable, staying 'Loyal and True' to the vision of growth and resilience. I hope the foundation we built will inspire future generations, proving that hope, unity, and determination can shape a brighter tomorrow.

About the Author

Dr. Sandra Zuniga Garza is a seasoned educational leader whose career bridges K–12 and higher education with uncommon depth and impact. With over three decades of experience, she has held executive roles including Assistant Superintendent, Chief Academic Officer, and Chief Innovation Officer. Across these positions, Sandra has led transformative initiatives — from launching dual language, STEM, and New Tech academies to building districtwide accountability systems and leading large-scale community safety collaborations.

Currently serving Southwest Texas College, Sandra is energized by the college's expanding mission to offer baccalaureate degrees in education with teacher certification — a development that aligns with her lifelong passion for cultivating future educators. Guided by a deep commitment to innovation, best practices, and data-driven improvement, she continues to champion institutional change and support student success.

Sandra has represented teacher education on the Board of Directors for the International Society for Technology in Education (ISTE) and has been honored with awards such as the Our Lady of the Lake University Agnes M. Gloyna Award for Technology Innovation in Teaching and Learning and the United States Presidential Volunteer Service Award.

She holds a doctorate in educational leadership and is an alumna of Texas A&M University–Corpus Christi and Kingsville, Angelo State University, and Sul Ross State University. Beyond her professional work, Sandra remains deeply rooted in her faith community, serving as a guitarist in the ACTS and Emmaus music ministries at Sacred Heart Catholic Church in Uvalde and as a proud member of the Delta Beta chapter of Delta Kappa Gamma International.

Above all, Sandra believes in the enduring power of people — that every educator, every student, and every community holds the strength to rise, transform challenges into triumphs, and leave a legacy that reaches far beyond the headlines.

www.ingramcontent.com/pod-product-compliance
Lightning Source LLC
Chambersburg PA
CBHW070641030426
42337CB00020B/4112